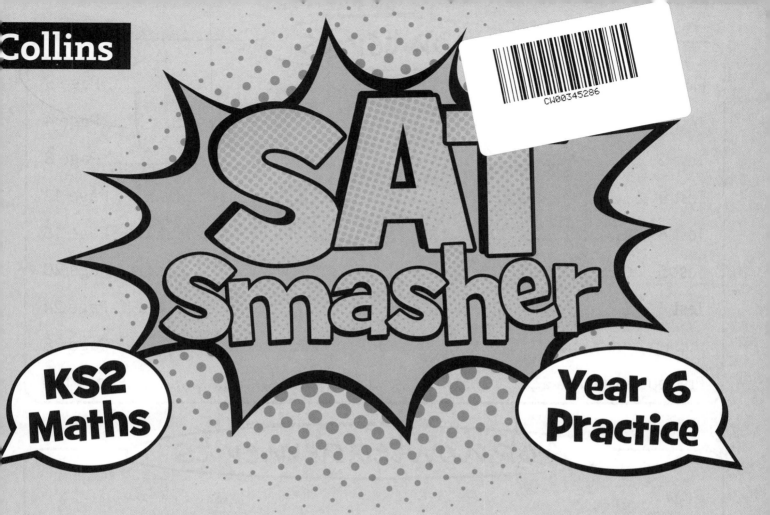

Ratio and Proportion

Russell Timmins

Contents

Acknowledgements

All images and illustrations are © Shutterstock.com and © HarperCollins*Publishers*.

Every effort has been made to trace copyright holders and obtain their permission for the use of copyright material. The author and publisher will gladly receive information enabling them to rectify any error or omission in subsequent editions. All facts are correct at time of going to press.

Published by Collins
An imprint of HarperCollins*Publishers* Ltd
1 London Bridge Street
London SE1 9GF

© HarperCollins*Publishers* Limited

ISBN 9780008259686

First published 2017

10 9 8 7 6 5 4 3 2 1

Commissioning Editor: Michelle I'Anson
Author: Russell Timmins
Project Manager and Editorial: Rebecca Skinner
Cover Design: Paul Oates
Inside Concept Design: Paul Oates
Text Design and Layout: Q2A Media
Printed in the UK

How to use this book

- You will need a blue / black pen or a dark pencil and a ruler (showing centimetres and millimetres).

- You **may not** use a calculator to answer any of the questions.

- Complete one test at a time. Test 1 is easier than the KS2 SAT papers. Tests 2 to 5 are the same level of difficulty as the actual tests and Test 6 is more challenging.

- Follow the instructions for each question.

- Questions are worth 1, 2 or 3 marks. The number under each line at the side of the page tells you the maximum number of marks for each question part.

- If you need to do working out, you can use the space around the question.

- Some questions have a 'Show your method' grid. For these questions, you may get a mark for showing your method even if the final answer is wrong.

- Cross out any answers that you wish to change.

- Remember to check your work carefully.

- The answers are in the pull-out section at the centre of this book.

- After completing all the tests, fill in the progress chart to identify what you are doing well in and what you can improve.

1. Albie makes a scale model of his house.

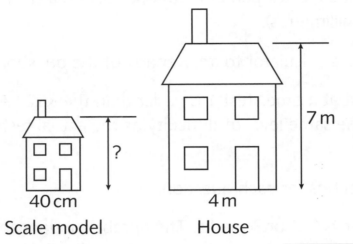

Scale model	House
40 cm	4 m

What is the height of Albie's scale model?

	cm

2. Tick **two** rectangles that are scaled versions of each other.

10 cm

8 cm | A | ☐

80 cm

10 cm | B | ☐

5 cm | C | ☐

40 cm

40 cm | D | ☐

50 cm

3. The large photograph is a scaled-up version of the small one.

35 cm

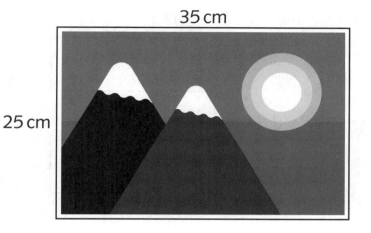

25 cm

7

?

Calculate the width of the small photograph.

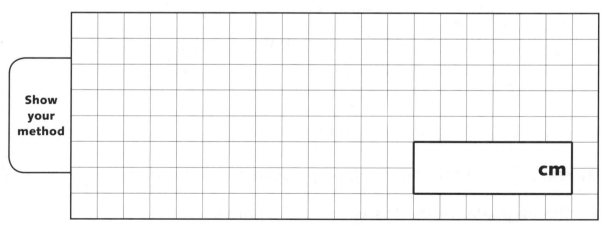

Show your method

cm

2 marks

4. Michelle earns £5 for every £2 that David earns.

How much would David earn if Michelle earned £20?

£

1 mark

How much would Michelle earn if David earned £6?

£

1 mark

5. Here is a triangle.

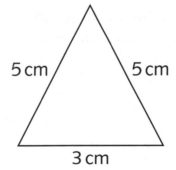

5 cm   5 cm

3 cm

Cleo increases the size of the triangle by a scale factor of 4

What is the perimeter of the triangle that Cleo draws?

cm

1 mark

6. Six toy cars cost the same as four toy trucks.
One toy truck costs £4.20

£4.20

How much does **one** toy car cost?

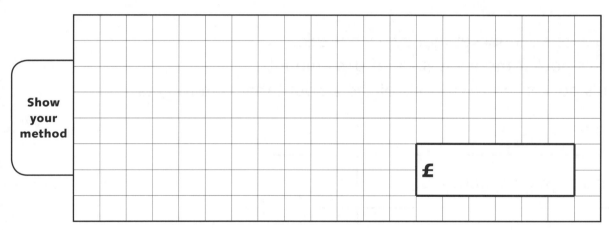

Show your method

£

2 marks

1. Hamir makes a 1:24 scale model of a real plane.
The model has a length of 30 cm.

What is the length of the real plane?

cm

1 mark

2. Rachael gets £8 pocket money each week.
Gareth's pocket money is 80% of this amount.
Dawn's pocket money is 90% of the amount that Gareth gets.

Complete the table.

Rachael's pocket money	£8
Gareth's pocket money	
Dawn's pocket money	

2 marks

3. Rectangle B is an enlargement of Rectangle A.

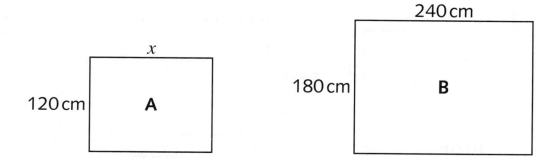

What is the length of side x?

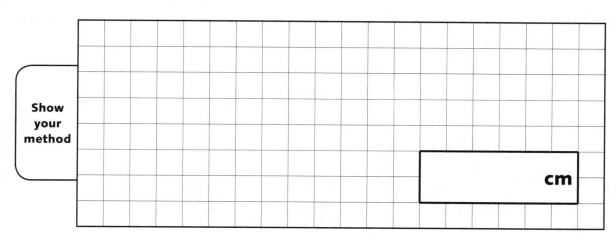

Show your method

cm

2 marks

4. The two hexagons are scaled versions of each other.

Write the lengths of sides x and y on the diagrams.

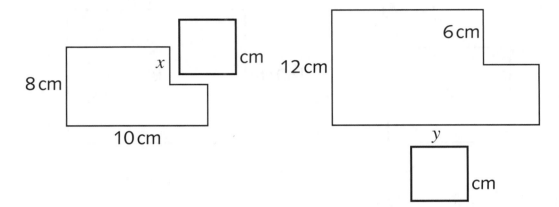

5. Cube N has sides of length 2 cm.
Cube M has sides of length 4 cm.

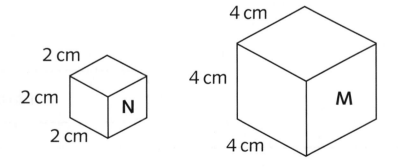

How many times greater is the volume of Cube M than Cube N?

times greater

6. The width of a rectangle is **three** times shorter than its length. The rectangle has a width of 6 cm.

What is the length of the rectangle?

cm

1 mark

What is the perimeter of the rectangle?

cm

1 mark

7. **1 litre** of red paint is needed to paint all the faces of a cube of side length **3 m**.

How many litres of paint would it take to paint all the faces of a cube of side length **6 m**?

Show your method

litres

2 marks

How am I doing? 😊 😐 ☹   Score   **/12**

1. A recipe states that 230 g of flour and 60 g of butter are needed to make 16 scones.
Jamie wants to make 40 scones.

How much flour does Jamie need?

| g |

1 mark

How much butter does Jamie need?

| g |

1 mark

2. Chris is 5 years older than Neil.
Their total age is 21 years.

How old is Neil?

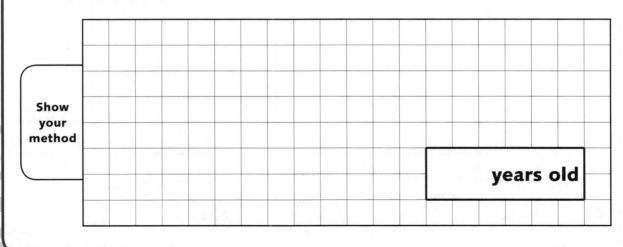

Show your method

| years old |

2 marks

3. The pie chart shows the ratio of ingredients used to make a milky coffee drink.

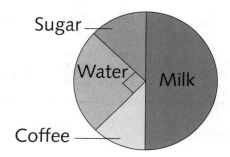

Sugar

Water

Milk

Coffee

The amount of sugar is equal to the amount of coffee.

What is the percentage of coffee in the drink?

%

4. A survey asks pupils whether they walk to school or travel by car.
88 pupils are surveyed.
The results show a ratio of 5:6 for walk:car.

How many pupils walk to school?

pupils

How many more travel by car?

pupils

5. Seven plane tickets cost a total of **£441**.

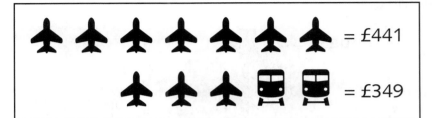

How much does **one** train ticket cost?

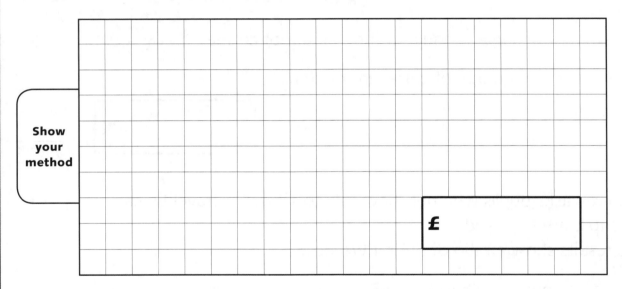

Show your method

£

3 marks

6. There are 40 teachers in a school. 24 of them are female.

What percentage of the teachers is male?

%

1 mark

Answers

For 2-mark answers shown with a star (2*), award 2 marks for the correct answer. If the answer is incorrect, award 1 mark for an appropriate method. For 3-mark questions, award 3 marks for the correct answer and, if the answer is incorrect, follow the guidance for awarding 2 or 1 marks.

Question	Answer(s)	Mark(s)	Content domain(s)
Test 1			
1	70 cm	1	6R1, 6R3
2	B AND C OR A AND D	1	6R3
3	5 cm	2*	6R1, 6R3
4	£8 £15	1 1	6R1, 6R4
5	52 cm	1	6R3, 4M7a
6	£2.80	2*	6R1
Test 2			
1	720 cm	1	6R1, 6R3
2	Gareth's pocket money £6.40 Dawn's pocket money £5.76	1 1	6R2, 5M9a
3	160 cm	2*	6R1, 6R3
4	$x = 4$ cm $y = 15$ cm	1 1	6R3
5	8 times greater	1	6R1, 6R3, 6M8a
6	18 cm 48 cm	1 1	6R1, 4M7a
7	4 litres	2*	6R1, 6R3

Test 3				
1	575 g 150 g	1 1		6R1
2	8 years old	2*		6R1
3	12.5% OR $12\frac{1}{2}$%	1		6R1, 6R2, 6S1
4	40 pupils 8 pupils	1 1		6R4
5	£80	3 (If the answer is incorrect, award 2 marks for an appropriate method with no more than one arithmetical error; 1 mark for evidence of an appropriate method)		6R1
6	40%	1		6R2
7	Accept any value from 30 to 40% Accept any value from 5 to 10%	1 1		6R2, 3S1
Test 4				
1	£14	2*		6R1, 5M9a
2	15 pupils Accept any value from 10 to 20%	1 1		6R2, 6S1
3	1.5 OR $1\frac{1}{2}$ litres	1		6R1
4	£3.50	2*		6R1
5	60% 16%	1 1		6R2
6	42 years old	2*		6R4
7	32 grapes	1		6R4

	Test 5		
1	£1,708	2*	6R2, 6R4
2	£17 £8.50	1 1	6R4, 5M9a
3	77 workers	2*	6R2
4	14% City / 12% Town / 24% United (pie chart)	1	6R1, 6S1
5	40% 27 fields	1 1	6R2
6	40p £1.60	1 1	6R1
7	£3	2*	6R2
8	4.5 cm OR $4\frac{1}{2}$ cm	1	6R3, 5M9b
	Test 6		
1	19%	1	6R2
2	160 km 20%	1 1	6R2, 6R4
3	260,000 people Answers will vary, e.g. $\frac{1}{4}$ is 25% and 13% + 11% = 24%	1 1	6R1, 6S1

4	Accept any value from 60 to 70% Accept any value from 12 to 20%	1 1	6R2
5	£10.50	3 (If the answer is incorrect, award 2 marks for an appropriate method with no more than one arithmetical error; 1 mark for evidence of an appropriate method)	6R2, 5M9a
6	60 cm 12 cm	1 1	6R2, 4M7a
7	(5, 6)	1	6R3, 6P2

7. 34 children in a class were given some strawberries, blackcurrants and raspberries to taste.

The bar chart shows how many children liked each fruit best.

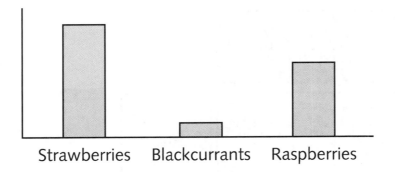

Strawberries   Blackcurrants   Raspberries

Approximately what percentage of the children chose raspberries?

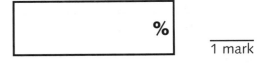
%

Approximately what percentage of the children chose blackcurrants?

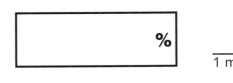
%

How am I doing?   Score   **/13**

1. A restaurant offers **two** set men...

The table shows the menus cho...
and the total bill.

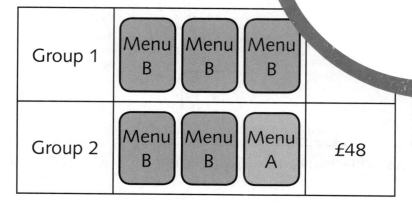

Group 1	Menu B	Menu B	Menu B	
Group 2	Menu B	Menu B	Menu A	£48

What is the cost of Menu A?

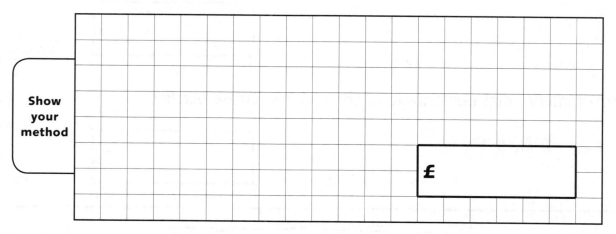

Show your method

£

2 marks

2. All the pupils in Class 6A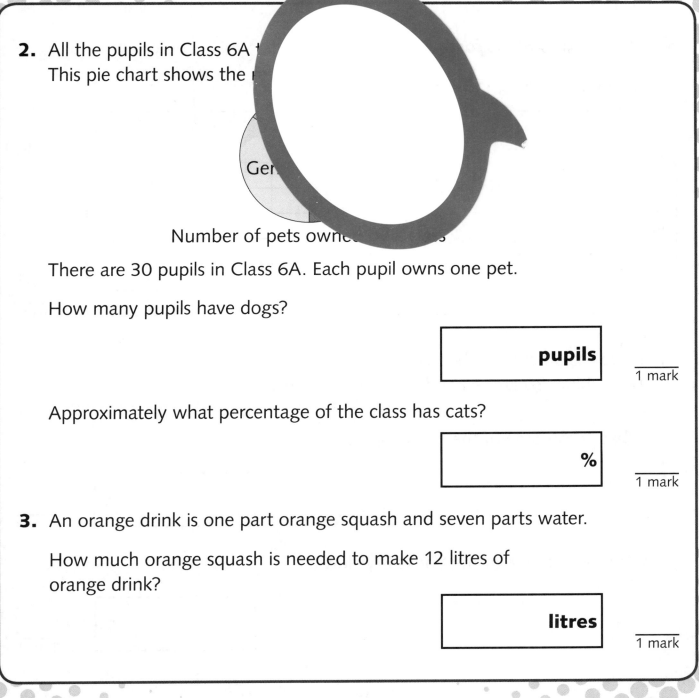
This pie chart shows the

Ger

Number of pets owned

There are 30 pupils in Class 6A. Each pupil owns one pet.

How many pupils have dogs?

pupils

Approximately what percentage of the class has cats?

%

3. An orange drink is one part orange squash and seven parts water.

How much orange squash is needed to make 12 litres of orange drink?

litres

4. Cheese costs £2.80 for 200 grams.

How much would 250 grams of cheese cost?

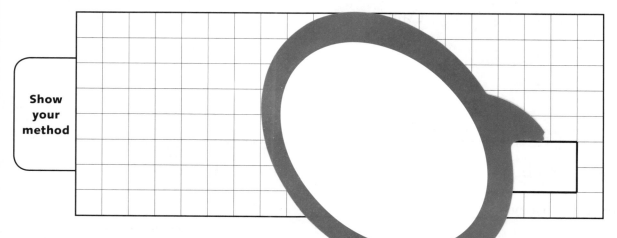

Show your method

2 marks

5. There are 50 exercise books in a box.
12 are blue, 30 are red and the rest are yellow.

What percentage of the books is red?

%

1 mark

What percentage of the books is yellow?

%

1 mark

6. Marion is 6 years older than Jada.
The total of their ages is 90 years.

How old is Jada?

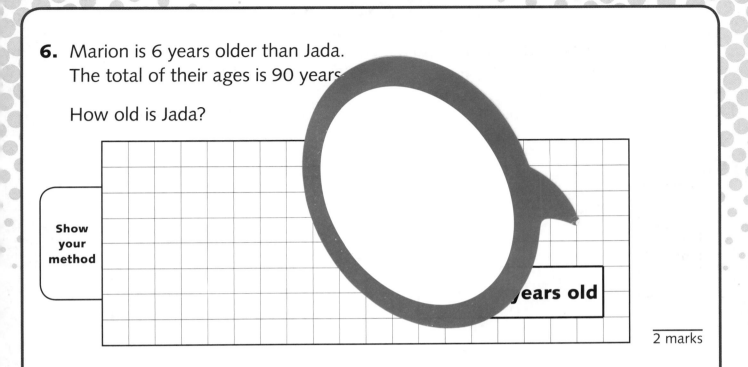

Show your method

years old

2 marks

7. Charlie and Paul share a bunch of grapes in the ratio 5:3

If Charlie gets 20 grapes, how many grapes were in the bunch?

grapes

1 mark

How am I doing?   Score   /12

1. An annual bus ticket for an adult costs £560
An annual bus ticket for a child costs 35% of an adult ticket.

What is the total cost for a family of two adults and three children?

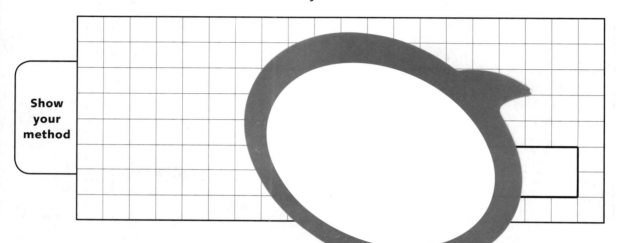

Show your method

2 marks

2. Donny has £6 less than Mona.
Donny and Mona have £28 between them.
George has half as much money as Mona.

How much money does Mona have?

£

1 mark

How much money does George have?

£

1 mark

3. 45% of the workers in a shop are male.

If there are 140 workers in the shop, how many are female?

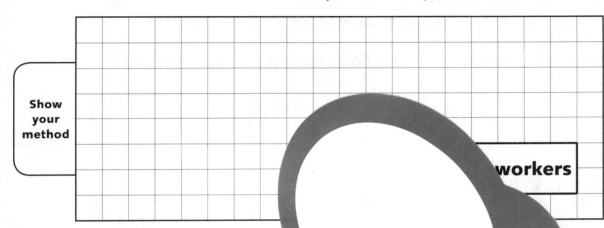

Show
your
method

workers

2 marks

4. A survey of favourite football t
12 Town fans and 24 United fan

Circle the chart that does **not** represe

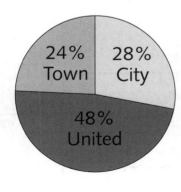

24%
Town

28%
City

48%
United

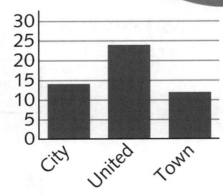

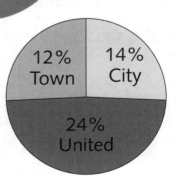

12%
Town

14%
City

24%
United

1 mark

5. A farmer has 60 fields.
15% of the fields are used to grow wheat.
24 of the fields are used to grow potatoes.
The rest of the fields are used to grow corn.

What percentage of the farmer's fields is used to grow potatoes?

%

How many fields are used

fields

6. 40% of the coins in a jar are 10
The rest are 20p pieces.
There are six 20p pieces.

What is the total value of the 10p pieces in the jar?

p

How much money is in the jar?

£

7. The price of a packet of biscuits is reduced by 10%.
The reduced price is £2.70

What is the full price of the packet of biscuits?

Show your method

2 marks

8. Write the length of the u

60°
3 cm   6 cm
30°

☐ cm

60°
9 cm
30°

1 mark

1. **Three** senior season tickets for Portsmouth FC cost £960 in total.
   A junior season ticket costs £60.80

   What percentage of the price of a senior ticket is a junior ticket?

   | % |

2. A straight road runs from Chichford to Peterwick, passing
   through Portstown.
   Chichford is 40 km from Portstown.
   Peterwick is four times this distance fro[...]

   Chichford

   ●————————●————————————
   40 km Portstown

   How far is Peterwick from Portstown?

   What percentage of the length of the road is the distance
   from Chichford to Portstown?

   | % |

3. The population of the West Midlands is 2 million.
The pie chart shows how this population is spread across different regions.

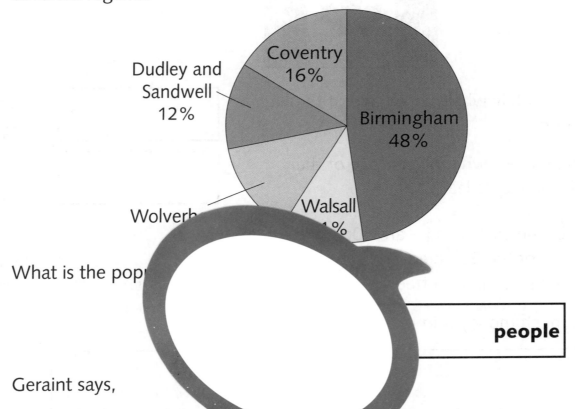

What is the pop

people

Geraint says,

'Looking at the pie chart, ￼he population of the West Midlands lives in Walsall and Wolverhampton.'

Explain why he is **incorrect**.

_____

_____

4. This is the flag of Canada.

Approximately what percentage of the flag is coloured?

%

Approximately what percentage of the flag is the maple leaf?

%

5. 20% of the coins in a jar are 50p pieces.
The sum of the 50p pieces is £2.50
The jar also contains fifteen 20p pieces and some £1 coins.

How much money is in the jar?

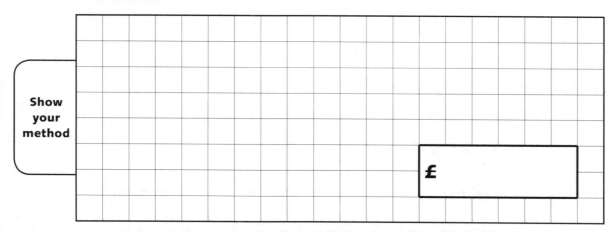

Show your method

£

3 marks

6. The perimeter of the regular pentagon is 20% longer than the perimeter of the rectangle.

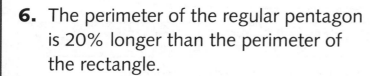

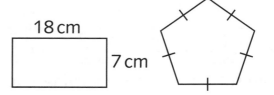

What is the perimeter of the pentagon?

	cm

1 mark

What is the length of one side of the pentagon?

	cm

1 mark

7. Triangle B has sides twice the length of Triangle A.

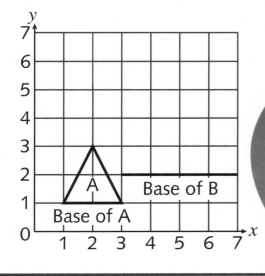

What are the coordinates of Triangle B's top vertex?

)

1 mark

How am I doing?   Score   **/13**

Pupil progress chart

Skills	✓ or X
I can solve problems involving two related quantities, where missing numbers can be found using multiplication or division.	
I can solve problems involving the calculation of percentages.	
I can use percentages to make comparisons.	
I can solve problems involving similar shapes where the scale factor is known or can be found.	
I can solve problems involving unequal sharing using my knowledge of fractions and multiples.	

What am I doing well in?

_____

_____

What do I need to improve?

_____

_____